ADVAITA

ADVAITA

THE TRUTH OF NON-DUALITY

In the words of
V. SUBRAHMANYA IYER

From the posthumous collections of
PAUL BRUNTON

Edited by Mark Scorelle

EPIGRAPH BOOKS
RHINEBECK, NEW YORK

All teachings are from:
'*Lights on Advaita: Selected Teachings of V. Subrahmanya Iyer*',
edited by Mark Scorelle, 1999;
Wisdom's Goldenrod, Center for Philosophic Studies,
5801 NYS rte 414, Hector, NY 14841;
www.wisdomsgoldenrod.org
With thanks to Kenneth Thurston Hurst
for his kind permission to publish these teachings.
The present compilation by André van den Brink, 2009
ISBN: 978-0-9725255-4-8
Library of Congress: 2009907423

CONTENTS

1

Philosophy:
the art and science of inquiring into truth

TRUTH is completely unified knowledge.

Those who say I am teaching only Shankara's system are mistaken. We want only *truth*, not authorities. My doctrine and position are not based on Shankara, but on inquiry into *truth*.

The whole of life has to be resolutely weighed and accurately observed in philosophy. We must ask: What is this world? What am I? Hence science is a necessary foundation...

Without knowing the nature of the world it is impossible to know truth. What is the use of trying to find your inner self before you understand the world?...

...Keen powers of observation are desirable and will help, not hinder your pursuit of truth. Take experiences as they come to you, do not run away from the world in ascetic fear of shyness of them. To say they are *maya* [illusion] without first examining them and inquiring into them thoroughly is to delude yourself. This world is common to all of us, therefore we must begin our inquiry with it and not flee. It is only *after* you have inquired into the nature of the objective world, that you should inquire into who is the knower...

In the old times Vedanta was taught, not by putting a pupil in a cave and telling him to sit quiet, but by taking him to a peepul tree and by breaking a seed off and showing it to the pupil, and breaking it into smaller and smaller fragments and pointing out to him the wonder of a great living tree growing out of the seed. Thus the *chela* [pupil] was shown the objective world first and taught to question about it.

Vedanta requires the mind to be active in order to examine the world and discriminate...

'Is this *true?*' is the beginning of philosophy: *Doubt* is the beginning of knowledge.

Advaita goes to the very root, where there is nothing more to doubt, nothing more to question.

Jnana [knowledge of truth] cannot come, if anything is left out. The *whole* universe must be included...

The chief purpose of analysing the external world is to discover that it is part of the ultimate reality and thus to enable us to carry on with activity from the highest possible viewpoint... To effect this discrimination we need an intelligence much sharper than the average, whereas too much religion and not a little mysticism drugs this intelligence...

Philosophy does not tell you to give up anything, but to know all.

How can anything be rejected? How can the world be renounced? Only those who delude themselves think so. Everything is *Brahman* and remains so.

The first thing we are aware of after waking, just as the first thing in an infant's experience, is the world outside. Therefore the first thing we ought to study is the world, not the self; to that *of which* we are aware, not that which *is* aware.

The *'Who am I?'* formula is useful as a first stage to show the illusoriness of ego and thus help the seeker to get rid of it. This prepares him to consider the higher question: *'What is the world?'*, the truth about which cannot be learnt by those attached to their ego...

Vedanta is the philosophy of verification.

Everyone says, 'This is a fact — I know — This is my experience.' None stops to doubt or to understand or to inquire as to what is 'a fact', or what is the definition of 'experience'.

...Vedantins take all the facts — science, religion, art etc. — and then ask of them, 'Which is the truth?' We collect as much evidence as possible, even contradictory, and then proceed to examine all of it. We are not opposed to anything but say, 'Analyse: How far is it *true*?'

...We do not know whether there is a God or not. There is no proof. If you mention God, you must prove his existence.

How do you know that you are related to God? Have you seen God? That he created the world, that he has manifested himself is merely supposed. It may be, but how do you *know*?...

How am I to know that what I believe is *true*? That question must prick the seeker.

If you have a belief, it is because somebody else believes it or the majority believes it, or it is your own experience. Is it religious authority or religious sanction, or is it based upon a *feeling* of certainty? Do you believe it merely because it works well, or is it true? If you ask the question of truth, it becomes a question of philosophy. Does your belief rest upon reason?

The purified intellect (*buddhi*) is reason.

Reason is the *common* ground for all humanity in modern times, whereas the appeal to scriptural relations reaches only groups. The great sages of Advaita knew that one day the world would throw up scriptures, hence they provided for the appeal to reason and met the objections of sceptics in their literature no less than those of religious believers.

Why do we appeal to reason and not to intuition, belief, authority etc.? Because of its universality, because all over the world and in all times there is only a single rational truth, because reason is the only way to obtain worldwide agreement amongst all peoples, nations, groups etc. Faith, intuition etc. varies tremendously in its imagined doctrines, scripture is interpreted by every man as he likes, but reason cannot vary in its truth.

...No assumption, no faith is needed by Vedanta, which demands *thinking*. People do not want to think: It is too troublesome. 'Why worry about philosophy?', they say... They do not want to be bothered to inquire.

Thinking is questioning experience. Something happens — A thing is seen or heard — and we ask: What is that? What do I see? What do I hear or feel? These somethings bring a message to the mind for inquiry. Reality is only inferred. Every object presented to us brings with it a question: What is it? This is the natural condition of the mind; it wants to get at the true explanation of a thing. This is the basis of truth.

Inquiry implies doubt, proof, evidence, so that even if God were to come and say that he is God, one would inquire into the truth of the statement. People are overawed by doctrines enunciated upon the authority of some famous man or institution or scripture. The one answer must be: How does he or it know? Truth must be *tested*. If it is true, it will survive the test and will bear proof. But everything else must inevitably find the props of pontifical authority to support it. How am I to *know* that this is truth? The first test is: Is it universally applicable? Which means: Will it be true in every other part of the globe? Will it be true in two million years' time? Will it be true for all people who pursue inquiry to the utmost extent?...

What is wanted in Advaita is thinking it out for yourself all the 24 hours and not merely reading books or hearing words.

The fundamental thing is to get a knowledge of truth *by your own experience and reason*. To say that Shankara writes the truth implies that you already know the truth and hence can certify Shankara's work. Until then you have no right to say whether his work is true.

Once truth is known, it can *never* be given up; you will *never* change your outlook again...

It is utterly impossible to unite the different religions or churches together. Even if such a thing were possible (which it is not), what are you going to do with the millions who are atheists or agnostics? They will not unite with the religionists. You can only say, 'Let there be tolerance', and that will be useful work. But you cannot bring them together in a unified structure. The only way to real unity is the search for truth.

For social purposes a religion is needed, because it unites a body of people, bringing them together in a common fold. Hence it is useful as a *value*. People however erroneously confuse social value with ultimate truth, for they jump to the conclusion that because it is *useful* in keeping people moral, for instance, a religion is *therefore* true.

Religion is essential for bringing up children in the way of good life. Therefore we say: Do not quarrel with religion. It has its valuable place for those whom it alone can help, who cannot even rise to the stage of mysticism. Those that criticise religion are quite correct as far as they themselves are concerned, but they are wrong where the world at large is concerned. It should not be taken away. To say the world can get on without religion is foolish.

The western world is giving up religion. That is inevitable owing to the decay of religious organisations. But their mistake is to rest satisfied with such a negative inner life and not to aspire to something *higher* than religion after giving it up.

Men are divided into three classes of intelligence. Those with lowest are given religion; those in the intermediate are given yoga; those in the highest are taught truth. We do not say religion and yoga are bad, but only that they are *steps* — not the highest level.

Peoples' minds have a natural tendency to run in various directions through pressure of attachments, environments, upbringing etc. Hence to retreat into a solitary place for yoga is good for them to stop this tendency, to get concentration. After that they should take up *vichara* [inquiry] and not remain in yoga. This is the order: yoga first, next inquiry…

To keep the mind unconfused and unconfounded by other thoughts than those pertaining to the theme selected for concentration: This is the principle and virtue of yoga.

Vedanta does not say that yoga has no value — everything in this world has its value — but that it is not the highest permanent value.

The body is valuable. It must be preserved and not ill-treated by asceticism, for it is our instrument of living. And whilst alive we know that we can reflect about truth. What happens after death, what opportunity to learn truth is there, we do not know. Truth is the object set before all human beings as the purpose of their lives. Hence we must care for the body, keep it alive and avoid death.

The facts of Vedanta are open to all, but the individual capacity to understand them will naturally vary. This is the only esotericism of Vedanta.

Vedanta says truth is reached by stages. Hence there is one version for children, another for the more advanced. It is not a question of 'esoteric', but of *capacity* to receive truth fit for one's stage. Hence it reconciles all versions, whilst pointing to the highest goal.

Indian philosophy gives a connecting link from primitive religion to the highest truth 'knowing which nothing remains to be known'.

First find out what stage a man is in. Does he want merely to get on in life? If so, prescribe religion. Does he want peace? Then prescribe yoga. Or does he want truth? Then alone should you initiate him into philosophy.

You must not yourself instil doubts in the minds of others. These doubts must arise of their own accord and only then may you answer them... To unsettle a satisfied mind is to lead it into bewilderment, with probable immorality as a consequence.

Philosophy is the search for truth. It is not opinion, not speculation, but reality which is verified by appealing to life as a whole.

Truth is the most important problem in philosophy.

What is the test of truth? The first test is its universality, as two plus two make four. The second test is that truth is beyond all possibility of contradiction.

Philosophers do not or cannot define truth. They may have many systems or theories, therefore any definition which they do give will not be acceptable to other schools and will be contradicted by them. Therefore we say that *first* an uncontradictable definition of truth must be found, before you can proceed.

I agree with you that the use of technical metaphysical language is not essential and is partly responsible for the metaphysicians' losing themselves in a forest of words, as Shankara says. Vedanta can be explained in simple terms. There is only one word students really have to learn the meaning of, that is the word '*truth*'.

The words 'verify' and 'validity' are two of the most difficult in philosophy. Every man may use them, but none knows what he is doing, for they imply the whole problem of 'What is truth?'...

Philosophy is not the totalisation, but the general interpretation of experience.

Philosophy is not making various theories about the Absolute, nor hairsplitting of words, nor imagining things: It is directed towards life and has the highest value in weighing life properly.

We need *all* phases of human thought and belief to help us, if we want a *complete* answer to the problem of human life. Philosophy is all-comprehensive, assigns a place for everything, and thus supplies this answer. It surveys the *whole*. If you exclude religion, you have no philosophy. If you take only religion, if you view life from a particular standpoint, again you have no philosophy.

Science is true so far as the world of science is concerned. Yoga is true so far as I sit quiet in meditation: The yogi's experiences are not lies, but truly described. All these are however only relative truths, true only from a certain narrow point of view. They come and go, they contradict each other, whereas we seek the supreme truth which is higher than all these, which is uncontradictable and does not conflict with anything else.

It is inevitable that thoughful people will have to come to the position which recognizes the twofold viewpoint: the immediate (*vyavaharic*) and the ultimate (*paramarthic*), for you cannot get absolute truth in this world. Time does not permit of proving every detail, hence we have to use belief to a large extent!... Hence the practical viewpoint is necessary for active life; it is the only possible one. But when you come to philosophy, then it is too defective and we must adopt the ultimate view...

Philosophy wants to understand the world as much as it was a million years ago as it is now, i.e. it does not depend on and is unaffected by personalities, the coming and going of *avatars* [divine incarnations]. That belongs to religion. Nor does it deal with the next world: It can deal only with the world in which we live. It studies truth irrespective of time (epoch) or locality.

The name 'System of Advaita' should not be used, because it is incorrect. *All* systems are ours, because there is non-contradiction in our view. The Advaitin feels there is no clash with others, he quarrels with none. He sees all their points of view... Our religion is *truth*, our philosophy is *truth*. Call it '*Search for Truth*' and leave out names.

Our position is not agnosticism nor atheism: It transcends both.

An Advaitin prefers not to state his case, but to let opponents do it first and [then] let him cross-examine them and expose their fallacies. By showing that all other doctrines are erroneous, he reveals that Advaita is left as the only alternative.

If you view a subject from your own standpoint alone, or from one technical standpoint only, you cannot view it rightly. Philosophy is the interpretation of the *whole*. Is it possible to get knowledge of the All? Vedanta says: Yes — not in its details, but in the sense of knowing its *essence*.

This philosophy is not mine, is not Shankara's, is not anyone's. Hence it cannot be labeled. It has come down to us from time immemorial. Who originally taught it is unknown.

2

Means and methods of inquiry

THERE are three stages of mental development: First, *instinctive*, which deals with sex, herd, nutrition and other animal instincts; second, *intuitive*, which arises from repeated human experience; third, *rational*. The last must be made supreme.

Logic is not the same as *reason*. There should be a distinction between them: Logic cannot know the Absolute; it is of intellect, not reason. Reason can know the Absolute. Logic applies only to the objective (seen) world...

Reasoning must not be confused with intellectual argument. The latter is used by lawyers for the logical building up of evidence of *seen* objects only, but the former is used in philosophy to refer to evidence of *all* the three states [of consciousness] (*avasthatraya*). Reason (*buddhi*) sees the appearance *and* disappearance of objects, including the ego, whereas logical intellect (*manas*) is limited to them alone.

Logic deals with causes, whereas reason deals with distinguishing between truth and falsehood.

Reason becomes *Atman* [the universal Self], when it is by itself, chained to no other thoughts. When it is so chained, then it is reason.

It is by the process of negation and affirmation that *Brahman* becomes the subject of reasoning. It is by reasoning that the identity of the *jiva* [the individual self] and *Brahman* is established. A direct knowledge of *Brahman* can never arise through any mystic initiation; yoga has no place in it. It can arise only through reasoning. Want of *faith* is the obstacle to religion. Want of *inquiry* is the obstacle to philosophy...

The two main features of science in which Vedanta is interested are *generalisation* and *verification*.

We should start with science to understand the world, but we must finish with philosophy, for the full explanation is essentially philosophical.

If science pursues its researches and does not stop, if it seeks constantly also to ascertain truth, it will be led into philosophy, because there is nowhere else for it to go.

Modern science is the starting point of philosophy. Science, however, deals only with one side, whereas philosophy deals with all: inside and outside, the knower and the known, for it is the knowledge of the *whole* of existence — that *all* is the universal Self.

...Modern science leads in the end to the discovery that the world is mind and that causality is non-existent. Precisely the same discovery was made by Gaudapada and Shankara. How? They had the spirit of science, the desire for ascertained facts and, being intellectuals of the highest order, saw the truth.

We must get at the truth without imagination. All the philosophies of the world are based on imagination, hence they contradict each other. A thousand persons imagine in a thousand different ways, each one believes that what *he* imagines is true. But where is the proof? People do not get truth, because they are attached to their particular and peculiar ideas. Attachment is the root of all evil.

Truth should not only be *known*, but it should be *proved, verified*. Advaita does not prove that there is *One*: It proves that there is no *second* thing!... This is the great difference between ours and other philosophies, no matter how similar their tenets may seem. Our method is the way of verification for every tenet: We want *proof*, not poetry. We do not care for either intuition or imagination, which is disastrous. A man may say, 'I have seen God; I have realised the Absolute', but he must *prove* it...

The value of meditation and yoga is to keep off extraneous thoughts. The average man cannot give attention to proper thought on Vedanta line, because he cannot keep his mind concentrated along this line: Yoga builds up the power to do so, hence it is useful as a preliminary process. We still the mind in order to get thought-control. But once this control is attained, then we must begin to *think*, to use one's mind again in a perfectly concentrated way and endeavor to understand the Vedantic truth...

Yoga's value is to *detach* the mind from this imprisonment in the body.

Yoga is intended to remove mental conflicts and further to keep out doubts and passions. It means keeping the mind always calm and alert. Yoga is a psychological training which is necessary before philosophical inquiry.

A sharpened intellect is necessary to perceive truth. Those who lack mental acuteness will not be able to grasp the meaning of the relativity of the three states. Such a dull intellect may, however, be perfectly adequate to handling the affairs of the world, and a man might be clever, astute and a successful businessman and yet remain incapable of grasping truth. The sharpness which is required is the subtlety and ability to move amid abstract ideas. Similarly the greatest scholar, however learned, may be unable to grasp it, because it requires real thinking and not mere memorizing.

Vedanta demands perfect calmness of mind, if you want to get truth, keeping out attachments and dislikes, anger and hatred from the mind.

Emotion cannot be killed, but it must be brought under the control and check of reason. Reason must be kept on top, as emotion often leads the truth-seeker astray.

That which dupes 99% of people is taking *satisfaction* for truth. Beware of that which satisfies your *feelings*.

If you do not take away the ego, the 'me', no proper inquiry into philosophical truth is possible, but only into religion.

The ego magnifies what it prefers or desires, thus distorting outlook and incapacitating it for truth.

The notion 'I know' prevents the minds of all from entering truth; it stops them from changing. Change is necessary in life, in practical as well as in cultural life. People must be ready to change, if they want to progress on any line...

You must be ever ready to criticize your own beliefs, to suspect your own fallacious thinking.

The mind must first be trained in the Vedantic way for a long time. Then only, when it reads such books as the *Brihadaranyaka* and *Mandukya Upanishads* does the true meaning of the texts become apparent. Hence we cannot give a sudden revelation of Advaita in one or two letters, or in an interview or two: A course of *personal* mental training must be undergone. Hence we say both the philosophical books *and* a living guru are necessary to the seeker.

The Vedantic method is *discussion* between teacher and pupils, not a dogmatic laying down by his authority.

You yourself must do the work of seeing truth by using your own judgment and reason. Nobody else, no guru can do it for you.

The right kind of seeker will accept and search for truth, whether it brings bitterness or sweetness, whatever it tastes like, for its own sake. He must be prepared to find God as impersonal and to lose his own individuality for the sake of truth.

Inquire further, do not be disheartened: Try over and over again. When you see that authoritarianism does not give you truth, you go further. You must have the determination to get at it. Experience tells you that every time you attempt, you progress.

3

The need of semantics

THE object indicated by the word and the word itself are one and the same in class, because both are mental, imagined.

First find out the *meaning* of words. You will find that they are simply mental images. These again are just your constructions and concoctions.

We must begin by examining the *meaning* of experience. Truth cannot be known before it is defined, before its *meaning* is understood. This does not mean indulging in speculation or forming opinions as to what may be true. It means inference based on life and experience in order to fix the goal of truth. It means that no important word should be received into the mind without asking of it what is felt in my mind, when I use this word.

Every man superimposes his own experience on others and *imagines* that their experience is like his. This is the fundamental fallacy of humanity everywhere. Thus you have never superimposed another man's pain. You can know the meaning of pain only by looking into your own *self*-experience. Hence *your* pain is personal experience, but your definition of the *other* man's pain is pure imagination. Hence your interpretation of a man's description of his pain is not in correspondence with it, but only your *imagination* of it. That is why Vedanta ascribes such importance to the question: What is meant by a *meaning*? Such a query goes to the bottom of the matter, for the answer to it is that we are *imagining* the whole world, including our own self. It is all nothing but our *idea*, and it all has nothing to do with the *Seer* of it, the *Drg*.

Define carefully the *meaning* of each important term used as it arises.

We must first define every important term we use, such as 'intellect', 'reason', 'time', 'eternity', 'consciousness', because it may carry one meaning to you and another to another man. Hence definition must *precede* explanation.

What do you mean by the word 'real'? What are the tests and characteristics of 'reality'? To reply that the external world is real alone is to ignore that this is based on the *feeling* of its reality. But you have a similar feeling in dream, hence it is useless to go by feeling. You must first find a definition that will hold. But people won't define; they want to go by feeling alone.

Reality:	*What we really are or what a thing really is, independent of man's conception of it.*
Truth:	*Man's conception of reality.*
Consciousness:	*That which becomes aware of everything else in the world.*
Ego:	*Personality or individuality as distinguished from the rest of the world.*

Reason:	*That which resolves contradiction and unifies knowledge.*
Intellect:	*That faculty of the human mind which detects fallacies and errors of man's reasoning in the waking state.*
Mind:	*The general sum of thoughts, imaginations, feelings etc.*

The word 'Absolute' is nonsensical and *Brahman* should never be translated by it. Yet the academic philosophers make this mistake. Ultimately there is only *mind*. If you think of the Absolute, then you are thinking of yourself as one and of the Absolute as another, i.e. of duality. Hence the Absolute of philosophy is not the non-dual *Brahman*.

The nearest English equivalent to the word '*Brahman*' is 'ultimate reality'.

The word 'One' is not understood anywhere except in Indian Vedanta. 'One' always means *two*, when analysed. Hence the *Upanishads* are careful to show they do not mean this monism, but 'One-without-a-second', i.e. Advaita...

A critical examination of concepts is required. As soon as a man utters the word 'God', we should ask what he *means* [by that] and let him make the word clear. Without understanding the word we are using, of what use or value is our knowledge? When we inquire, we shall find how difficult it is to define exactly words which are commonly and superficially used in knowledge, such as 'space', 'law', 'cause', 'truth' etc...

Nay, we have to go deeper in philosophy and ascertain the meaning of '*meaning*'.

A 'meaning' is an *idea*. Therefore it exists in the *mind*. Until you look into a man's mind, how can you prove that what *you* mean by a word is what the other man means? How do you know that *his* meaning is the same as yours? For practical purposes of everyday life we do not trouble about these things, but for knowing the truth of things we have to inquire into their meanings...

Is the term 'mind' or 'consciousness' or 'awareness' a word? Yes. Has a word a meaning? Yes. What *is* a 'meaning'? Something which you imagine. Then how do you know whether your imagined meaning is correct? You refer to your own experience to see whether it corresponds. But this means that you are referring to *your thoughts* only.

...You use the word 'move': The world is 'in motion'. But what is it that makes it move? This is a semantic analysis of vital importance. What do you do, when you try to understand this word (or any other)?... What is meant, when you say a thing has 'changed'? Let us go to the root of the matter. The answer is that you cannot have a meaning for a word, unless you have it in your own experience. The ideas of 'change' and 'motion' must originally come to you *within yourself*, otherwise it is meaningless. Hence we say philosophers must learn the *meaning* of 'meaning'. This is the Indian term '*anubhava*' ('within your experience')... You see the world in yourself. Everything that you see in this world is in yourself.

What is meant by a 'meaning'? It is a *thought*. Hence a meaning is only a *drsyam* [an object *seen*]. This in turn implies a *knower* [a *seer*] of it. Hence there are *two*. Hence it is not Advaita. This is what I call the meaning of 'meaning', which must be got at.

How do you get a 'meaning' for words? What is meant by 'understanding' a word? Each time you get only an idea. To use the words 'truth', 'reality', *'Brahman'*, is merely to form an *idea* of them, i.e. a *drsyam*, an object. Sages use such words only to help others rise from lower to higher steps, not to *explain* them. Each dual statement is used to demolish another, to point out the absurdity of another, as one thorn is used to pull out another. So the guru has to use those incorrect statements of truth to help the student rise to the final statement which, being non-dual, must be unspoken. Hence discussion and learning about truth are not useless, although they cannot yield finality, because they are all riddled with duality, with objectiveness (*drsyam*), i.e. contradiction. The best explanation is *silence*. So long as talk proceeds, the words are helpful, but still they are in duality… So long as we speak or write we can never leave duality. Hence the only genuine expression of Truth is perfect silence. He who utters the word *'Brahman'* does not understand it, for in that moment he assigns a *meaning* to it, i.e. an idea, imagination.

The ultimate value of semantics is to show the futility of all words in the quest of truth, thus causing you to go *beyond* words into silence where alone *Brahman* can be got.

You may know that all books may be thrown in the dustbin, because they are all ideas, but this does not mean they are useless. They can be used like one thorn picking out a second one that is embedded in the flesh. So words as expressive of ideas, although useless for knowing *Brahman*, are useful for removing ignorance and error which bar the way to such knowledge.

We begin by inquiring into the external world. We inquire into the nature of internal worlds, i.e. minds, ideas, thoughts etc. We inquire into the meaning of words we use. Finally we ask: What is that which is unchanging and real?

4

Perception and idealism

WHAT happens when you see an object? Light rays are transmitted from it to your retina. The object itself does not impinge on your eyes, only the rays. After that vibrations or impulses travel up the optic nerve to the brain. What happens to the nerve during this passage of vibrations? Rapid oscillations! The sensation reaches the brain. What happens next? The sensations are converted into ideas or images. What converts them? The mind! At this moment alone — not before — do you become aware of the object. Moreover all you know of it is the idea or image which now registers in the mind.

You see John. What have you done by seeing him? His picture has fallen on your retina. That picture is say half an inch long. He is six feet tall. Hence you did not see *him*, but the picture and hence it is the *mind* which has seen him. It has formed an *idea* of John. When I compare my idea of John with John and form a judgment, I have only compared one idea with another idea. *It is impossible to see John in himself.* Hence the impossibility of accepting the 'correspondence theory' of truth. The same applies to touching John and any of the other senses. It is the *mind* which really senses. Does the mind come directly in contact with John? No! Therefore it merely forms an *idea* of John: John is only an idea…

Roughness, smoothness etc. are qualities which cannot exist without a mind to perceive them, i.e. they cannot exist unperceived. Therefore the individual object to which these qualities belong cannot also exist unperceived. It is the *mind* that presents everything to us. Whatever is seen is seen by the mind.

The insoluble gap which exists for science between the physical sensation and the mental awareness of it disappears for the Vedantin, because on inquiry he finds that he never saw a physical sensation: It was really a *mental* sensation, an idea in the mind which you may easily copy into a second similar idea.

...The image's impression is carried by the optic nerve to the brain. Cut off this nerve and the man sees nothing. This proves the nerve is necessary to communication. How? It vibrates and sets up these vibrations in the brain. Science has to stop at this point, it cannot explain. Nobody knows how this vibration is converted into idea. The mind constructs from these vibrations an image. This establishes beyond all doubt that it is the *mind* that constructs the image, the picture. Thus idealism is irrefutably proved... What is the original stimulus for the vibration? The mind asking itself this question can only answer itself by inferring or assuming an object outside. But never forget that mind has never come into *direct* awareness of an object. There is no proof therefore that a separate object exists outside, but the mind habitually *assumes* it to be there from the beginning. It has in no case seen it directly. What then is the stimulus? *This very question involves unconscious assumption that the outside, separate object exists.* Those who say we must have previously seen the object in order to form an idea of it subsequently, we reply: Did they ever see an object independently of the mind? Is it not the *mind* that first gave information of the thing, of its qualities? The object, the rays of light and the whole sensory organ-nerve-brain process is not known by the mind at the time, it is only imagined *afterwards*, when it analyses the way in which its knowledge arises. All the mind really and undubitably knows is the picture, the idea which it forms itself. All the rest has been imagined by it: *All this is itself an idea*. The object as cause of the idea is unprovable, but is assumed by the mind at the very start of the process, it itself remaining unaware that it has started with the assumption. It wrongly takes the separate object for granted. Whatever else is offered in place of the object as cause, such as God, must also be something unknown and unknowable, for anything known can only be an *idea*: The mind knows only its *own* constructions. This effectually kills materialism, for no matter is thus findable. Mind alone is...

When the nerve vibrations are present, mind knows the thing. When they are not there, the mind is unaware of any object. Hence the scientific account of sensation and perception is purely inferential, although based on sound facts as far as they are known. We are never conscious of how sense impressions are manifested into perceptions, but we *infer* the process. The only certain thing is the mind's own activity.

If you go on inquiring into the physical processes of sensation, your inquiry lands you into thought, the mental process. Science cannot discover the relation between physical and mental for the simple reason that the physical *is* ultimately mental. It has set us an artificial, non-existent problem and vainly strives to solve it. So long as duality grips the mind, the latter seeks to establish relations. Hence it tries to find out the relation between mind and body, a hopeless task.

Objective or ontological idealism teaches there is a real outside object of which my mind tells me, and my mind could not form the idea unless the object were there, whereas subjective or epistemological ideal-ism teaches that I do not know whether there is any outside object other than my mind. I neither deny or accept it. I say simply that I do not know. Even if it existed, I still know only what my *mind* tells me about it.

Injure the optic nerve and although an object is be-fore you, you will see nothing. This is proof that we have the sensation first and only afterwards become aware of the object. When we receive no sensation, we never become aware of the object, as in sleep. Why? Because the object is an *inference* which we make from the sensation itself.

The fact that objects are inferences drawn from sensation is obscured partly because of the rapidity with which the inference is drawn and partly because people never stop to inquire and reflect as to what is going on when they see an object. And partly because they will not think matters out to the logical end owing to their innate belief in causality, predisposing them to look for a *separate* object as the *cause* of their impres-sion of it. When everything is found to be but mind, whether it be object, seer, senses, nerves, impression etc., then all becomes a unity and there is no room for cause and effect, because *there are no two things.*

The old query, 'How can a nerve vibration be converted into an idea?', has broken down, vanished, as latest science has solved it by saying that the two are not separate, that mind and matter are *one*.

…Vedanta says that if we have to recognize the original independent object as being an idea, then the intermediary parts of the sensory process, i.e. eye, nerve, brain, must logically be ideas also. What happens therefore is that we return to our starting point and discover that the original outside object which gave rise to the sensations is our perception of it, that the thing *is* the thought perceived: The image seen in the mind was also the object supposed to exist outside and to cause the image to arise. How so? *Because* we began with an assumption that there was an object independent of the mind, and we continued to assume that the thought which arose was independent of this object, so finally we have to decide that the object itself must be still there outside. But our initial assumption was unwarranted: It is only our imagination at work and the truth is that there is no duality of thing and the perceived percept of the thing. Rather there is only *one* entity, i.e. the thought itself. Much of this confusion has arisen because of the use of the word 'idea' of things, for we habitually believe that ideas are internal and do not grasp that they may be external too, that therefore space is as illusory as matter. The essence of this explanantion is that the whole thing is traveling unconsciously in a circle. We start with an idea and end with precisely the same idea.

What we start with we call 'outside object' and what we finish with we call 'percept'. Our illusion lies in thinking the two are different. They are not, but one and the same.

The term 'thought' must be used differently from the term 'idea'. A thought is any passing fancy or any feeling or any desire which comes and goes *within yourself*. An idea is not a thought in the above sense, but a sensation of some object which is apparently *outside yourself*. Thus you will form an *idea* of a table, whereas you will have the *thought* of removing the table from one room to another.

Why do we not *feel* this world to be idea? Reply: Because of the strength of our attachment to the body, of our identification with it, which in its turn is due to not having inquired into the nature of the body and discovered its constantly changing nature. We have to take the Witness attitude to see the body as a fleeting appearance.

Unless you grasp that the world is an idea, there is no other way of proceeding to the higher truths of Vedanta.

5

Change and illusion

I F you see anything, it is bound to pass away. How is it seen? By the mind. Therefore the mind alone produces ideas of a world. Realise all things pass away, that just as the dream world passes away, the waking world also passes. It is not, as yogis suggest, the *non*-seeing of the wall which reveals it as *maya* [changing, illusory, unreal], but on the contrary the *seeing* of it. For the perception of objects is a *mental* act which involves the mind and its ideas alone.

There is *illusory* existence and *real* existence. The highest intellectual inquiry is regarding the external world, the world which is seen in the waking state. 'What is the nature of the world which I see?', is the first question with which you must start. We can show that the same principle that *seen* objects are *unreal* applies to the waking no less than to the dream state...

The world scene is constantly changing. The stars, moon and everything changes. *Maya* asks: What is the *meaning* of this change? People ignorantly attribute a mysterious power to *maya*, but it is simply change in its true meaning. *Maya* is that which appears and afterwards disappears. People accept the fading of a flower without inquiry. Only when you ask what has become of its vanished colour, you are asking the meaning of *maya*.

In order to understand the problem we begin by teaching that the imaginary snake dissolves in the rope. Now at a more advanced stage we teach that, as the snake was *mind*, where could it have been lost but again in the *mind,* which means that it was not *really* lost. Hence all that can be said of it (and of the world) is that it appears and disappears. There is no destruction.

Seed which becomes plant, plant which becomes tree, tree which becomes seed again: All this is *maya*, i.e. impermanent, changing.

As Bergson and the Buddhist idealists teach everything is idea, that each idea is fleeting. Thus this table lasts only a millionth of a second, but the continuous multiplication of the same idea of the table fuses the countless ideas of it and gives the impression that it is lasting for twenty years. Time itself is only an idea, as Kant shows and Einstein implies. It is precisely the same with a cinema picture of a table: It shows for a half-hour the same table, but actually it consists of thousands of separate pictures fused together. So our world of ever-changing flux *appears* stable, because the multitude of ideas follow with such rapidity as to yield the impression of stability.

The individual is a bundle of memories, desires etc. What are memories and desires? Something imagined. Therefore the individual self is entirely an imagination.

If the body is a reality, where is your body as a child, when it ran about, was different in appearance and different in structure? It has vanished. Then what was it at the time? What else but an *idea*? And how can a thing which changes and disappears be *real*?

Death means the conversion of forms considered real into ideas.

The 'unreality' of the world means that everything is continually *changing*, that it is *momentary*.

...While we are actually seeing the world, it would be madness to deny its existence. *Maya* does not mean that. We see change, i.e. ideas come and go. Experience shows that one thing changes into another. Only foolish people say that anything can become non-existent. So the whole world must remain existent in some way or other and cannot totally disappear.

Maya means that which *appears* to be real, but is unreal. Also that which disappears, when you know its real nature.

...In your use of the word '*maya*' remember it is not the constant change of the world, but the illusion which arises *as a result* of the change.

What do you mean by 'change'? It means the coming in of an idea and the going out of another idea. The moment the mind begins to think, change occurs. Thus the succession of ideas is called change. In deep sleep there is no idea and no change either. Ideas always indicate change. You never know change, unless the mind is thinking.

Advaita does not deny the existence of the world, it only asks of what substance can the world be. The Advaitin sees the world as much as anyone else.

...When you know the waves as water, then it [water] is always there. But when you think of them only as *waves*, then they will seem to vanish. Hence if you view the world of objects as *different* from *Brahman*, then you will see them disappear and appear. But when you go to the truth, the imagined differences will vanish and the world unity as *Brahman* will remain... When you know what the reality is, then you are unable to think of the appearance as being different. The essence remains then, even though the forms change. The world that we see, this body and this mind, are all of one stuff. This explains the mutual interdependence and interaction which science discovers.

All that we know is the visible world. That it is ever-changing we learn only after inquiry. Until then we wrongly ascribe permanence, reality to it. Yet, although the ascription is wrong, the sense of reality is there, because it is *within ourselves*, in *Atman*, and we *superimpose* it on the world that is visibly seen.

Though we start with the doctrine of change, continuous and everywhere, we end with the opposite doctrine that there is no change in reality: Nothing is born or dies.

'Illusion' does not mean the non-existence of anything. Those who do not understand Vedanta teach this wrong definition.

Advaita does not deny the existence of external objects: It denies their reality.

The world has existence. Even the snake seen in an illusion has existence, even appearances have existence. It is therefore absurd to deny the existence of anything experienced. What we ought to do, however, is to ask ourselves: What is *meant* by 'existence'?

People always make a mistake in confusing *reality* with *existence*. Appearances may exist, as a snake or a mirage, and yet not be a reality.

'Illusion' means that it does not affect the reality. The snake illusion does not affect or change the rope. You have not become a man, you are what you always were: eternal *Brahman*.

Vedanta does not dispense with externality. Take the case of dream, when the 'fear' is inside and the 'tiger' outside. We perceive both internal and external. The external world is reduced to ideas and the ideas are reduced to *Atman*. Vedanta is neither idealism nor realism.

People who use the word 'external' ought to define it first. They speak of an *external* world. External to what? Is the body external or internal to the mind? If the body is included in the world (as it must be, because it is built up from food, water, air taken from it), then if the body is internal (as it must be to the mind), the whole world must also be internal.

You may see the mirage as water, you may see it a second time after realisation and [then] know that it is *not* water. But, even as a *jnani* [knower of truth], you will still *see* it as water, but *know* it as otherwise. The seeing is not altered, only the knowing. Similarly the world will still be seen by the sage, and its appearance will be exactly like its appearance to ordinary men. There will be no difference in the visual sensation, but the *jnani* will also evaluate it as unreal.

You may put a stick in water a thousand times, but it will always be seen as bent, even though you know it to be straight. Similarly you may know that all the individual forms are a unity, *Brahman*, and yet you will continue to see them as separate entities, even though you are a *jnani*. This is the higher lesson of the study of illusions.

...When you think of the past, you think it in the present. I get the idea of present only by distinguishing it from the past or future. It is an *idea*. Can you experience this present really? What is meant by 'the present'? It involves distinction, it depends on past and future. Both these do not exist. Therefore the present does not exist as such. The conclusion is that all time is but idea, imagination... When can you draw a line and say this instant is the present? In reality you cannot do this, you cannot 'hold' the present. Time is only an idea, and all events therefore are ideas with it. The present *appears* to exist and yet it does not. Hence we call time *maya*...

There is no such thing as a measure of time. Close analysis will reveal that all our measurements based on planetary revolutions are ultimately nothing else than mental impressions. Time is how we *think* it. Ein-

stein has begun to point to this truth without however realising the tremendous consequences which
must ultimately follow, when this path of analysis is
pushed to its logical and fullest extent. Thus, by com-
paring the dream state with the waking state we may
perceive how, as dreams occur in the mind, time is
purely mental. The same discriminations apply to the
notion of space also…

If time proved to be but an idea, then eternity must
be the same too. What is eternity? That which is without beginning or end: an idea merely. Because who
can say what is going to happen the next minute, let
alone all eternity?… Hence even eternity and time,
as ideas, must collapse or disappear. At this point
people will fear to go further. Eternity consoled them
with the thought of surviving death. If it vanishes,
they feel lost. But no, something is left: To *whom* have
these ideas come? To the Self. In *whom* do they appear and vanish? In the Self. Hence the Self as Witness
still remains. Now, the world was shown to be but
an idea. All ideas disappear into the Self. Hence the
world disappears into the Self. Or the Self contains
the whole world. It is the Witness of the three states
[of consciousness]: It *is*. Why add predicates? It em-
braces everything. What cause then for fear? This is
the *Upanishad* teaching. Even the idea 'eternity' disappears into the Self and is contained by it. Why fear?

The snake-rope illusion doctrine is the first stage
of inquiry, a novice's preliminary step. But the higher
stage reveals that the illusion itself is reality. Only be-
ginners talk of the world as illusory, the wise make no
distinction and find reality in everything. You give up

name and form at an earlier stage to discover later on that they too are *Brahman*. However, the first step of negating the world is necessary to help the student. It is equivalent to the melting process, of throwing many gold ornaments into one mass in order to learn what gold is in itself, apart from its forms. Once known, we may recast the mass back into original shaped ornaments and ever after know them as gold alone. You eliminate differences tentatively by taking away all forms in order to know eventually that everything is *Brahman*.

Our philosophical teaching is not that unity exists in multiplicity, but that unity *alone* is: Multiplicity does not exist.

6

Mind, the ideation of consciousness

W HAT is it that prevents us from seeing the world in the Self? The error of thinking that the mind is in the body instead of the reverse. The mind cannot be confined to the body, we do not know its extent: Nobody has seen it inside the body.

Do not imprison yourself in your own creation by imagining the mind to be limited to the body. Just as space fills both the inside and outside of a jar, so mind permeates you and the whole world outside.

We cannot say where the limits of the mind are. The mind is like a mirror and our body is like a reflection in this mirror, just as all other objects are. When you know mind is unlimited and that your body is limited, then it follows that the latter must be *within* the mind.

The European idea, as soon as the word 'mind' is uttered, is that it means the mind of an *individual*, whereas we Vedantins mean by it 'that to which anything appears'. This is an important and vital difference. Ours is thus a *common* mind.

An idea means that you imagine. In Vedanta the word 'idea' stands for 'mental construction' − not that which the ego has constructed, but that which is constructed by the mind which itself sees the ego: the *common* mind.

The critic who said, 'The world is an idea: Why don't you think a chair and then go and sit down on it?', is making two errors: First he thinks the idealist takes his own body as real and only the rest of the world as an idea; second he does not know that it is not the *individual* mind which creates the universe and its objects, but that mind which itself sees the individual, in short the *common* mind. The individual has no powers to make the universe. That which makes the universe makes the individual also. This point is very difficult to grasp...

...It is not *my* idea, but the common mind which imagines that and this person. You may have seen the birth and death of other beings, thoughts and feelings, but you have never seen the birth and death of the Knower or Seer. You may imagine it, but even that implies the imaginer. In other words *you* must be there *before* thinking. Hence in this sense the Self is termed 'the Unborn'...

What is mind? It is that which can assume any form.

When we talk of the body-mind problem, we necessarily refer to the *individual* mind. But when we talk of the matter-mind problem, we refer to the *universal* mind. Thus we must be careful to understand the use of the terms 'mind' correctly.

...If you can cast away the ego-consciousness, the individual mind is the same as the universal mind.

All objects and creatures are mind alone. In advanced Vedanta you convert this statement into, 'are *Atman* alone'.

…All these [scriptural] quotations prove that Advaita teaches that mind is none other than what India calls Self, *Atman*, Universe and *Brahman*.

The mind has never been separated from the objects and creatures seen in your dream. Therefore at no time has the mind itself been separate from them. Even in the waking state no object is ever separated from the mind. Ideas must stand somewhere, be created of something, and this is mind. We use the word 'mind' here instead of *'Brahman'*, for it is easier to see that all things, being ideas, are made of one stuff: mind.

…Everything in the world is within the mind, but you see it as outside. All movements of consciousness are only apparent. Is the dream body really running? Consciousness is immovable, for space itself is an idea within it. You can imagine an object moving from place to place, but the consciousness itself does not move… All thoughts of the world are within the mind: When there are no thoughts of the world, it is not seen. This shows that the world is in the mind and *is* mind. Hence there is no real duality of a real world and a real observer. Even the Himalayas are only a notion of consciousness, are only imagination. We take the world as real and separate because of our previous attachment to it for the sake of satisfying our desires. The ignorant here take the idea to be real. Nothing has gone out elsewhere, nothing has come into the mind, wherein everything happens, from elsewhere. Nothing is produced, caused: *There is no second outside Atman...*

When you know the body is only an idea, you can look forward to its death, the greatest of all sorrows, with equanimity. For when an idea disappears, it goes back to its source, [it] cannot be lost. The mountain you saw in dream has vanished. Where? Back into the mind. The form is not different from the essence, body from Self. Hence there is neither coming or going. That which is *is*, and forever.

You have seen the birth of a man's body, but you have never seen the birth of his consciousness. Hence we call the latter 'unborn'. From the Advaita standpoint the word 'substratum' has no meaning. You speak of a substratum only, when you think of something *other*, then it also [has] a quality etc. This means a *second*, hence duality... There is only one consciousness and we can't limit it to two individuals or speak of them as different — for we are obsessed by the ideas of body alone. Duality is with the body; in the consciousness, the unseen *Atman*, it disappears. If you are always thinking of variety alone, you see duality! If you think of unity, you perceive that. Hence realisation depends upon your state of mind...

When someone is awake, we usually call him conscious. But pure awareness still exists, even when he is under anesthesia. We must separate *pure* consciousness from the *ideas* in it, such as the ideas of waking objects and environment.

We cannot prove positively that consciousness has vanished in sleep, you can only show it negatively. For you cannot know the limits of consciousness, you cannot posit where it starts, stops, vanishes etc. This is what Europeans do not understand. We use the word 'consciousness' to include non-dual states like sleep, whereas the west uses it only for duality states. Westerners do not grasp that consciousness can remain without objects, as in sleep, and yet be conscious still: This is *contentless consciousness.*

The western idea of consciousness implies an objective relation, whereas the Vedantic idea is that it is the unrelated Subject alone.

Those critics of idealism who ask, 'What was the world before human minds existed?', ask an unaskable question which is quite out of order. The first fallacy is that matter existed before mind. How do they know this, unless the mind is first there to tell them? Science now admits, moreover, that we do not know when the mind came into existence. Hence no critic can definitely say it came later than the material world. We can only say that consciousness is *fundamental* and everything else is *derivative.*

That which you know best in the world, that which is nearest to you, that of which you can never be free, whose existence is supremely certain, is your consciousness. You may doubt anything else, but you directly perceive yourself. Hence we begin the study of Vedanta with the study of consciousness... Just as to explain the nature of gold we take a single gold ornament first and then tell you that all gold ornaments are made of this same single material, so to explain the nature of the unknown *Brahman* we start with something known and familiar, viz. consciousness, which you have in the three states [of waking, dreaming and deep sleep], and proceed step by step from that onwards: You know your *Atman*, it is directly perceived; thinking implies a thinking capacity, i.e. a thinker: This *Atman* is your consciousness. After showing that this consciousness, this Self [*Atman*] is *Brahman*, we then explain that everything else is of the same nature, which should enable you henceforth to understand all else. Moreover everyone has and knows this consciousness, therefore it is a universal datum. It is something which everybody can grasp, not merely some occultist or mystic, therefore there is no mystery-mongering in our study.

The whole world is of the nature of consciousness. This you can realise by the illustration of dream. And the world-consciousness is not different from your own: They are of the same substance or stuff. The objects rise and fall back in this consciousness like waves in the ocean.

Waking objects, on account of their being similar to dream objects, are unreal, because they are *perceived objects*. This is important and must be understood. For what is it that perceives? It is the mind. What is it that the mind has in it, when it sees an object? An idea. Suppose anything existed outside or different from the mind, what is it that would have to tell you about it? The mind. As in dream the mind is that which informs you of the existence of objects, i.e. it is only an act of the *mind*. Those who say things exist apart from or independent of the mind talk like children. Where is the proof? This principle must be thought over a million times, until you thoroughly grasp it. It is only the mind that makes a thing perceived, hence objects are *mental states*.

No philosopher, whether in India or Europe, has even been able to define the meaning of 'mind' and 'consciousness'.

How long, high and broad is your mind? You do not know where it begins or ends. You cannot say it stops here. Have you seen your own mind or anyone else's mind? Yet people talk of *my* mind, *his* mind, as though each mind was numbered and separated. Science now says that the mind is not limited; we cannot measure it or allot it to separate individuals; that it is everywhere. Is your mind within your body or vice versa? If you say your mind is within the six inches of skull, that implies you have seen and measured it, which is a lie. *No man has ever seen a mind.* We may say, however, that every man has got his own *thoughts*, his own *ideas*, which are not in another man's mind. But the mind itself is all one, though thoughts may be many. All the external places, cities, bodies are within the mind.

We say the mind is everywhere, because we cannot determine its limits. But what is 'everywhere'? It is space. What is space? An idea, i.e. mind. Thus you see that when analysis is carried to its last, which is the principle of Vedanta, we find the mind is really indefinable and indescribable: That it is the *Drg* [the Seer].

How is it, critics say, that every man has a different mind, yet you say there is only one consciousness or *Atman*? Reply: There is only one sun, but it will cast a million separate reflections on the ocean; or a fire will throw out a hundred sparks. In the same way understand the Self.

We need to be careful in using the word 'consciousness' with westerners, because they apply it only to the awareness of objects, whereas India has specific Sanskrit words whose equivalents in English do not exist, for pure, transcendent, objectless consciousness, inclusive of deep sleep, dream and waking.

The Vedantin does not say there is no external world. He says only that the external world (of objects) as well as the internal world (of ideas) are all of the same stuff, i.e. mind.

The external wall is dependent on my mind. Unless my mind is active, I see nothing and the wall does not exist when my mind is not there, as in sleep. To say that the wall is still there in sleep is unprovable, hence unacceptable to Vedanta.

...Thus you return to the fundamental fact that the existence of a thing depends on your *knowing* it, otherwise you merely infer it. But inference is not direct verification. If you say the wall existed unperceived while you slept, this is not correct. It was only *after* waking that you *inferred* it had existed, i.e. your mind told you so, which is again turning the wall into an idea!

How to think the world ceases to exist when asleep? The problem exists only for those who think the external world *already* exists as real and who think their body also exists as real. When one sees their unreality, the problem collapses.

Mind when active is called mind! When it ceases to be active, i.e. sinks back and is only itself, the essence, the substance or material, it is then called *Atman*, the Self, the Seer.

The mind itself is the *Drg* [the Seer], it can never be seen. Hence you cannot rightly speak even of 'my' mind. You know nothing of it directly...

There is only one mind. Each ego, each 'I' is itself an idea in this universal mind. This explains how personal separateness is an illusion.

People think that the 'soul' or 'spirit' is something different from the mind. They believe that the mind is really two. This is the confusion among Dvaitins, Vishishtadvaitins and Europeans. If 'soul' has any meaning, if 'spirit' has any meaning, so long as you *think* of them, they are merely *ideas*. No, mind is the highest: It is consciousness, *jnana*.

If you analyse all the objects in the world, all the bodies, you will find that ultimately there is only one substance, one thing which changes into all these different forms. We then go further and say that this unitary substance can be traced to consciousness.

7

The Self, the Seer of the seen

I T is impossible to get to the Knower, the *Drg*, before it is understood that the world is an *idea*.

There is no such thing as 'knowing the Knower'. That knowledge implies two factors, and the
Knower, not being something to be seen, can never be
known as such. When we speak of 'relation', we deal
only with the *known* world. When the known goes,
we [can] say that, because we actually *see* the known
going. But we can never see the Knower go; we can
only say, 'I do not know', about it. We cannot speak
of the known without the Knower... We cannot con-
ceive the *Drg*, the Seer or Knower, because we can say
nothing about it without making it an object. It cannot
be pulled down to the level of the *drsyam*, the seen...

The Self is not a thing unknown to anyone at any
time. Let a man think. As soon as a thought comes,
there must be a Knower there *before* in order to know
that he is seeing a wall etc. The *Drg* exists *before* the
thought appears or the thing is seen, otherwise neither knowledge nor sensation could happen. When
can you say the *Drg* is *not* there? It is always there.
Even if you say it can be reached only at the end of
a long path, it is impossible for it to be ever absent,
even while you say this. The Knower alone makes it
possible for you to know anything at all.

'Though thus quite self-evident, easily known, quite near, forming the Self, *Brahman* appears to the unenlightened mind as unknown, very remote, as though he were a separate thing', says Shankara's commentary on the [*Bhagavad*] *Gita*. Those who do not look at the Seer, the Witness, and perceive that it is the only thing that neither comes nor goes, are deluded and turn outward, towards things objective which run away. So long as the mind only runs from one object to another, from one idea to another, impermanent and unreal, they ignore the *Atman* and are [thus] ignorant. Where is the time for them to think about the Witness?

...Thus three words need analysis: 'experience', 'knowledge', 'self', or confusion results. This analysis is the *Drg-drsya-viveka* task [the discrimination between the Seer and the seen].

The body is what I know, what I perceive; the perceiver is distinct. The body is a *drsyam*, a thought. I am not my thoughts. The answer to the query, 'What am I?', is, 'I, the *Atman*, am *pure knowing*'. When there is duality, doubt comes. And so long as a man thinks there is a *second* thing to be obtained, he can never be happy, because [then] duality is always there. The *jnani*, on the other hand, regards nothing as different, i.e. as a second thing, and therefore escapes this unhappiness.

That which becomes conscious of all the things contained in consciousness, is the Seer, the *Atman*, the Knower. You have never seen the *Atman*, for he is never an object. Hence logic, inference, cannot be applied to him, because intellect, logic, is for the objective world and waking experience only, the state where we infer effects from causes. The greatest mistake is to think of the seen as yourself, to confuse the object with the subject. There is no proof that the Seer is confined to you, yourself, or me, myself. It is universal.

...The inability to see [ignorance] is not in the perceiver. But there is something which comes and goes, which hides and prevents you from 'seeing'. This 'something' is like a veil. What prevents you from seeing is not yourself, it is a fault of the *mind*, not the Seer. The mind is only an instrument which you utilise. If this ignorance were a property of the Seer, it could never go, but it is not. The ignorance is something that comes and goes, but the Seer is untouched by it.

There is no connection between the Witness and the ego which appears and disappears, is happy or miserable, which the Witness sees... The witnessing consciousness remains unconcerned.

...The critic assumes that you are an ego-centric solipsist who alone exists and created the world. But we do not fall into solipsism, because we make the ego also an idea and do not assume its reality as does the critic. Mental ideas may be objective.

Once you understand the ego, you will have understood 90% of Vedanta. You must learn that the ego is different from consciousness.

What am I? The 'I' disappears every night in sleep, so what is the use of being attached to it? It is illusory.

The Witness itself is *jnana*. It is quite erroneous to say it *has jnana*. It *is* thinking, seeing. The distinction between objects and the knower is produced by itself.

Every thought is an object, *drsyam*. That which cannot be cognized by any thought, which is beyond all doubt, because it is that which is the ultimate consciousness of the doubter, that is *Brahman*.

...I am the Witness of the 'I' also. If you do not grasp this point, you cannot understand Vedanta. When you see a table, your awareness must have been present even before [seeing it], otherwise how could you have been aware of it? This awareness is the real *Atman*, not the ego. The awareness is there always, even when the table is not seen. Nothing could ever be thought of, if awareness, the capacity to think of it, were ever absent at any time. When are you free from awareness? If you say that, at any moment, it is *not* [there], then somebody must have been aware of this 'non-awareness'.

Who knows the waves? The ocean knows the waves.

The first stage is to regard all things as *drsyam* and separate yourself from them. But this is tentative and is for those who still labour under the ego-complex. But the next and higher stage is to see them all as

Brahman. Then you no longer turn away from them. All is then 'I' [i.e. *Atman*].

The man who knows thoroughly that everything in his life is only a changing *drsyam*, that *drsyams* are but transient thoughts, if he then identifies himself with the *Drg*, he can stand unaffected by loss, because he knows that he himself, the *Atman*, can never be lost or lose anything in itself. Knowing the *drsyam* as part of himself, he no longer considers it as a *drsyam*. Such a distinction exists only when inquiring. The ignorant man *imagines* he is related to objects, *imagines* there is a causal relation with them and then *imagines* his sufferings because of their [the objects'] transiency. He foolishly believes that anything can go away from his *Atman*, because he separates himself from them.

The body is part of the external universe. It holds its own reality and keeps you from seeing the world as idea. All the 24 hours you think the body is real and occupy yourself with it. But as it is part of the *seen*, and the world is *seen*, you take the latter to be real also. Only when you perceive that *both* these, that whatever object the mind sees — even your own body — is only an idea, is your own mind, hence your own Self, then you can go further and find that that very Self in its essence is *Brahman.* That truth reveals all objects and persons as One.

How far does the *Atman* go? Where is it limited? I am the same being everywhere. Its separateness from others is only imagined (as through the body). All other human beings are within this Self and non-separate from it. If you think of being different from others or from God or from suffering people, you can never re-alise the Self. This is true *ahimsa* [non-violence]. Only those who know it refuse to inflict injury on others.

Everybody says 'I', but everyone sees differences in each 'I'. Remove the differences and take the common factor of all the 'I's. This is the real 'I'.

You will know that everything is *Brahman*, when the 'I' goes. Everything is immortal, being *Atman*. It is impossible to die. Though thou art only the *Drg*, you identify yourself with the *drsyam* — [with] the 'I' which is dying every day in sleep, the 'I' [which] van-ishes every moment in the waking state also — not to speak of the dream 'I'. The 'I' idea comes and goes, no idea of it is permanent. Think ever that you are the Witness of the changing 'I's. Use one thorn or idea to get rid of another thorn or idea.

That the *Drg* is common everywhere is easily proved, because everyone refers to himself first by 'I'; he adds his personal name only secondarily. The 'I' is always spoken first: *I* am here, *I* am doing this. This is true in all languages, used by all men as the primary answer to any questions. Personal names come later. Why does every man use the word 'I'? If he is *essen-tially* different from others, why does he use the same word 'I'?... Why does a woman use the same word 'I' as a man, although she knows that she is so different in many respects?... The whole of humanity is classi-fied under the name 'I'. What is the common feature of this multitudinous 'I'?... That common feature is which Vedanta seeks. In short we are inquiring into the meaning of the word 'Man'...

...That which exists really is *Atman* only. The 'I' which is changing is wrongly identified with the unchanging *Atman*, the *Drg*-'I'. How do you know? Because the former 'I' changes, appears and disappears. Mind alone is the cause of bondage and freedom. We do not rely on immortality because it is said so in the *Upanishads*, but because it is actually experienced. Of what use are quotations? Vedanta appeals to facts.

The difference between us and other schools is that they have the erroneous belief that there is some Reality *apart* from us which is unborn and eternal, whereas we know it to be our very own *Atman*.

The 'I' is the first *kalpana*, the first idea the human mind imagines.

The first thing in ignorance, the root of it, is egoism. So long as you have 'I'[ego], it is useless to think you can find truth. This is the opposite of all other religions and philosophies which take the individual self for real and build up promises or attainments on it.

Most people shrink in fear of losing their ego. This is due to ignorance, for the truth is that the 'I', the ego, is also *Brahman* and, as *Brahman*, cannot really be lost.

Getting rid of the ego does not mean losing the sense of individuality. It [ego] may be felt, experienced, but it must be known for what it is: an idea, a *drsyam*. We cannot deny the ego being there, but we can understand what it really is: a transient *drsyam*. Let the ego exist, it cannot be abolished. But don't be deceived by it into seeking its satisfaction at the expense of truth.

The moment that you give up the ego, you will get the 'lightning flash' and know that you are everywhere (not that you are *acting* everywhere), and that everything is *in* you. Like that other flash between two [successive] thoughts it is something extremely subtle, hence hard to detect, demanding extreme concentration.

The individual self is only an *idea*... There *are* no two selves: The personality never exists apart from its ultimate entity, *Brahman*.

'Individuality' has no meaning: That is the point. The *Drg* is that which has no limitations. All ideas regarding limitation are imagined. We have to catch that which is *between* two ideas in order to eliminate ideas. I am the 'Knower' in all.

The 'I' is a compound of a changing factor, ego, and an unchanging factor, consciousness.

...To talk of 'shifting the consciousness from ego to *Brahman*' is wrong, because your consciousness is *already* in *Brahman* and therefore does not need shifting.

You must see your body, all other bodies, everything, as *ideas* which you know as *Self*: This is realisation. It can come only *after* you know that the seen is not separate from the Seer.

If the universe exists in me, then when the idea of 'me' also goes, then the universal illusion goes with it. This is the most advanced position in Vedanta. In other words a separate universe no longer exists for the *jnani*. Even the superimposition of the world on my mind is then seen to be illusory: The *jnani* knows in this higher stage that superimposition is only mind, that nothing else is.

8

Avasthatraya:
coordinating the three states of consciousness

I NDIAN philosophy: Its uniqueness relies on the
totality of experience by coordinating the three
states of waking, dream and deep sleep [*avasthatraya*] — not on waking alone like other philosophies,
arts, sciences and religions.

Vedanta takes the *whole* of experience throughout
the universe that you get in the waking state. It [then]
asks the question: What is the meaning of dream and
sleep?...

The student must pass first through the stage of scientific proof from waking world facts for idealism: He
must know that things are *ideas*. Then only is he ready
to pass to the higher stage of studying *avasthatraya*.
Here dream shows what powers the mind possesses
to manufacture whole worlds, to create externality
and internality, i.e. space. Sleep shows what power the
mind possesses to reabsorb, store and later reproduce
all the ideas of the world, space etc. Finally, having
shown all this, *avasthatraya* clinches and carries to final culmination the idealistic theory learnt from waking state facts and shows what the nature of mind is,
what ego is, and that everything is not only ultimately
one or non-dual, but also *not apart from yourself.*

There is no way to discover that the world is
idea except by modern scientific analysis of matter.

Avasthatraya cannot be used for this, it is only an illustration in this connection. *Avasthatraya* is not needed to prove idealism. Scientific analyses of sense perception such as [those of] Russell, Eddington and even Berkeley up to a point, form the only real proof. *Avasthatraya* can merely illustrate idealism, although it is the only proof, when you step beyond idealism. Scientific analysis of sensation is quite enough to prove idealism. When the world is known to be idea, *avasthatraya* is the only proof of the world being *in* you, and the only way to understand the nature of *Atman*. Idealists fear solipsism quite rightly, because they make the mistake of putting the world in the ego, not in *Atman*. They have seen only 'ego-solipsism', not '*Atman*-solipsism' which is the truth. Proof of idealism can only be got from science. There only can you see the world and yet know it to be nothing more than idea.

Advaita begins by using dream as an illustration. Then it proceeds to use it as an analogy. But in the final stage it proceeds to ask what, after all, is the difference between our waking life and dream life?... We can find no difference whatever between waking and dream. They are both of the same character, i.e. they are both *mental*.

Dream is the same as the waking state so long as it lasts. Whatever applies to the latter belongs to the former also. Hence when I say intellect is reason confined to waking, I include dream in the latter.

It will be a great error to write that the world is a dream: It is not. The correct statement is: The world is *like* a dream. This is because both dream and waking worlds are *mental* constructs.

Deep sleep has been given you by nature to show how in *jnana* the whole universe goes back into you as idea.

What is the philosophical value of sleep? Has nature given it to you merely for physical, utilitarian purposes? No. There is also a higher value. When you think of a *meaning,* when you get an *idea* of non-duality, you are still in the world of duality [and] you begin to imagine, '*Brahman* must be like this', or, '*Brahman* must be like that'. Thus you merely get your own imagination back. You can raise no questions in deep sleep, therefore, to help you to understand *Brahman* aright, nature gives you deep sleep. But it is a help only. Sleep is not *Brahman,* however.

Why should men have sleep? Nature wants to teach you that it is possible to have a state where there will be no imagination, no duality, no fear. In sleep no questions can be asked, no answers given, there is nothing. Questions can be asked where imaginations are possible, i.e. in the waking state. The secondless state is always present, even now during the waking state. When the mind has learned to inquire properly, it finds this non-dual state even during waking, as it is never absent. It is wrong to take sleep as *jnana* or *moksha* [liberation]. The case of sleep is given only as an illustration or analogy...

Deep sleep is simply having no ideas.

How is dreamless sleep known? No ideas and no objects were present then, hence it is only known by negation. In the same way the pure Self is also only known by negation.

Think of a coconut tree idea; next moment a mango tree idea. What happened *between* these ideas? I do not know. Why do you remember the ideas? There is a discontinuity of thought between the idea of a horse and the idea of an ass. What was there *between* the two ideas? One idea is not the same as another, the mind distinguishes them. Then what is there between them? This shows that 'sleep' or the absence of objects intervenes even in the waking state.

It is quite impossible to know that there is a waking state, unless you have dream and sleep to compare it with (like contrasting colours). Hence knowledge is only possible, when you have differentiation. And since the *Drg* is the Undifferentiated, it can never be known in the ordinary sense of being distinguished from anything else, as the three states. You cannot talk of the *absence* of objects, when there are no [other] objects for contrast.

Those who object that the means and ends of waking are different from those of dreams, and therefore they are not on the same level, ignore that you have time, space and causal relation in both states. These three things make the waking world real to you and are its chief characteristics. Similarly they give the same sense of reality to dream. They say: Waking is real and dream is illusory. We say *both* are illusory.

It is essential to inquire into the presence of objects before we can understand the truth of their reality. The presence of objects is known only in terms of their absence, i.e. the colour black is known as black only in terms of contrast with the colour white. Hence reality is to be known only as distinguished from *un*reality. In deep sleep the entire universe disappears from consciousness, i.e. becomes unreal. Therefore, the different states are really *relative* to each other. In truth, when the mind gets the consciousness of reality, there is no distinction between the three states.

I say that the waking state *includes* the others, because it is only when you are awake that you know dream and sleep exist. During dream itself you take it for the time being as though it were waking, and you are unable to know otherwise. The necessary contrast to enable you to distinguish between the states can only be effected whilst awake. Then only you can perceive that waking is only a state that comes and goes; you cannot perceive this during dream or sleep. Hence realisation can only be effected in the waking state. Hence too the need for the west to study *avasthatraya*.

The relativity of the three states: You could not know black as black, if white did not exist. If only one colour existed, you would never be aware of that fact. Only by existence of another opposite or contrasting colour do you know (it). Similarly you would not know waking as waking, if life were always waking state. You know the waking state exists because of the existence of the dream state, by way of contrast, and [because of the existence] of deep sleep. Therefore the three states are present together and are always present.

A quarter of a rupee is included in a one-rupee piece; half a rupee is already there in a one-rupee bit. Therefore the quarter- and half-rupees are merged in the one-rupee bit. When you have a whole rupee, you don't inquire: Does it contain a quarter or a three-quarter rupee in it? You know that both are present therein. You can by inquiry convert, merge or dissolve all the parts of a rupee in the whole one. Similarly you can show that waking dissolves in dream, dream disappears in deep sleep, and the latter merges in *Turiya* ['the fourth state']. This is done by converting the world of material objects into an idea. Europe is now learning this first quarter and has yet to learn what becomes of these ideas, and what becomes of deep sleep, i.e. two more stages or quarters. In this way everything — 'All this', as the *Mandukya* [*Upanishad*] says in the first *shloka* [verse] — becomes *Turiya* or *Brahman*.

Turiya is not the 'fourth' state: *Turiya* is that in which all the others are merged, or it may be called the Witness which sees the other three states.

Turiya is not a state or condition: We can only experience the three states [of waking, dreaming and deep sleep]. *Turiya* is present always: That which knows all the three states is itself changeless.

When we utter the word 'sound', how can we understand the *meaning* of sound? It is only by distinguishing it from soundlessness that we can understand sound.

All sounds are got from soundlessness. Similarly all the states are got from *Turiya*, corresponding to soundlessness. We have to merge waking into dream, then merge dream into deep sleep, and finally we have to merge even this into *Turiya*.

Where did the sound go after utterance? Whence did it come?… Since all sounds come out of *me*, I can only use the term 'self' for it. Similarly all the world comes out of myself, as it needs *me* to recognize it. Just as all spoken sounds come out of me and go back, I can only say a soundless state in me was their source. You cannot say it is a *non*-entity, because the sounds come out again. Similarly you can't say that you don't exist in deep sleep, because you re-emerge [from it]. The big Self existed then. Buddha meant, when he said the self did not exist, that the *little* self alone did not exist.

If you subtract from your experience everything which is known, then you have *Turiya*, objectlessness. To understand this, note that sleep is [also] objectless, but you get no knowledge of it except in the waking state… If you learn the way to negate ideas, which is possible, you may reach reality. But you can see it only in a lightning flash of a second, it is so quick. You know it has come, but cannot catch it. The moment an idea arrives, you know that it was preceded by the blank. Hence the interval between two thoughts is *Turiya*. Therefore you have to examine your own mind with tremendous watchfulness to get it. The three states come of their own accord, but *Turiya* is seen by intensely sharp vigilance only. *Turiya* is the *absence* of the three states. It is always present, but must be probed for. It must always be there, because it is implied by the presence of the three states. Were it not there, you could never think. *Turiya* only can get [you] the meaning of existence and non-existence. When you can realise within yourself the non-existence of objects, that is *Turiya*.

The three states are known in the waking state, not in dream or sleep. Hence you must detach yourself from them whilst awake, if you are to realise *Turiya*. In the waking world alone can we get *Brahman*. The mind has to be so sharp in order to catch the meaning of the word 'state' as applied to waking, for if it sees it thoroughly, it will at once know it is in *Turiya*.

Because deep sleep is followed by dream and waking, it is called the seed or causal state... It is a *state*, something which comes and goes. The objects of each state are included in it. The *jnani* detaches himself from them [the three states], sees them coming and going, and thus remains in the ever-present non-dual *Turiya*. Everyone knows these states are transient, but everyone does not detach himself from them. It takes time to realise the truth of *avasthatraya* as it does to realise non-causality, although you may perceive them intellectually. The moment you know that the three are only *states*, you know the *Drg* which is *Turiya*. But you have to know this continually...

Until you become fully aware during the dream state that you *are* dreaming, you are not ready for the higher Vedanta teaching which gives *jnana*. You must begin to practise to perceive your dream experiences so as to become conscious that it *is* a dream in the dream state itself. This will cause the waking self to grasp the idea that both idea and object constitute the whole category of existence. All is mind. If this memory that what you see and what you think as well as your individual self are ideas [persists], then that is *jnana*.

Knowledge of *Atman* is true knowledge [*jnana*], not merely the absence of duality as in *sushupti* [deep sleep], where you don't *know* that it is *Brahman*. *Jnana* is to see the world and say that it is all *Brahman*. Even the Himalayas are *in* you. Control of the mind is essential to know the unreality (not the *absence*) of the phenomenal world. *Sushupti* can't be equated with *jnana*.

In sleep there is no positive misery or pleasure, but only *absence* of misery and pleasure, i.e. absence of duality. But a *jnani* must have the knowledge of the absence of duality even in the waking state. Then only there is realisation. We must distinguish between absence of duality and the *knowledge* of the absence of duality.

Because we are not aware of any other thing in sleep, we have to admit that every idea, both internal and external, has merged into the mind during sleep as undifferentiated consciousness.

The fact that sleep is a *drsyam* is proved, because we know it as being sleep only *after* we are awake, i.e. when it is past and gone, i.e. when it has vanished. And is it not the characteristic of a *drsyam* to vanish, to change? It is only a temporary state, whereas *Brah-*

man is permanent and not a state. Moreover it is the activity of the *buddhi* [reason] which brings the understanding of *Brahman*, and the *buddhi* is inactive in sleep. Finally the sleeper sees nothing, whereas the *jnani* sees the world, sees *Brahman*, even in waking.

All the three states are *Brahman*. To think that waking is not *Brahman*, whereas sleep is *Brahman* is an error. Similarly to say that *Turiya* is *Brahman* and the three states are not is error: All is *Brahman* without exception...

9

Realisation of truth is the removing of ignorance

T HAT alone is called truth which is a fact that can
never be changed under any circumstances.

The definition of truth according to Vedanta is non-duality.

Wherever there is impermanence and transiency,
there is necessarily duality. But that which *knows*
these things are passing away, that is the pure non-
dual consciousness.

Non-duality does not mean the non-existence of a
second thing, but its non-existence as *other* than yourself. The mind must know it is of the same substance
as the objects.

The nature of truth is to be free from contradictions. We approach nearer and nearer truth as we find
less and less contradictions. The only thing which is
so free is non-duality.

Truth is not only that which is beyond contradiction, but also that in which there is no *possibility* of
contradiction. Such a state can only be realised as *non-*
duality, where there are no two persons. The illustration for that is deep sleep, but sleep is not the ultimate
reality; it is merely an analogy. The *Brihadaranyaka
Upanishad* teaches, 'If you think there is another entity, whether man or God, there is no truth.' This is the

teaching since time immemorial of those who have inquired into truth.

Why is *Brahman* beyond speech? Because whenever you use a word, it implies a meaning, a thought. When you get a thought, there must be a witness of the thought apart from it. The thought is not, cannot know and does not grasp its witness.

If *Brahman* is beyond thought and speech, why study books or listen to lectures on Advaita? Reply: On the principle of using one thorn to prick another out of the flesh and then throwing both away, we use these books and lectures to remove wrong thoughts, misleading words, to get rid of erroneous assumptions about *Brahman*, thus removing our ignorance.

What is the difference between *Atman* and *Brahman*? When you dissolve all the world into ideas and then the ideas into yourself, knowing they are ultimately *in* you, that is *Atman*. When you actually see the universe before you and know that it is the same as yourself, that is *Brahman*. When you are dreaming and know that the dream pictures of cities, friends etc. are yourself, that is *Brahman*. We have first to pass through the stage of discovering *Atman* and then only can we attain the stage of discovering *Brahman*. Nevertheless it must not be thought that the two are different: Both *Atman* and *Brahman* are one and the same thing, but viewed from two different angles.

It won't do to say reality is only *within* you. You must know that this table, this book is also reality. All that you see is reality.

The Seer in me, the Seer in him, the Seer in someone else, are all one and the same, not separate from each other. Nobody has ever seen more than one Seer.

We do not seek God in the quest: Our only object is truth. If we find that truth happens to be God, all right, we must accept it. But we cannot prejudge the issue.

We are not opposed to God, we are not atheists. But we want God free from our or others' imagination, as He is in truth, as He exists apart from human imaginations. Imagined Gods cannot help us. We do not say God is not there. He is, but not as you *imagine* him. We want the God *above* all imaginations: That which exists as Truth. Hence we do not use the word 'God'. It will be misunderstood.

Liberation (*moksha*) is not something to be got after death. It means liberation from ignorance whilst alive.

…The definition usually given by pundits and yogis in India of the word '*moksha*' as meaning 'liberation from the cycle of transmigration' pertains to the lower or purely religious sphere. This doctrine is on a lower level, because it is based on the reality of the ego. The Vedantic interpretation of the word is 'liberation from ignorance'.

If one has to enter the kingdom of heaven, then God may one day get annoyed and throw one out again. Why not? Who can read God's mind? No, anything that begins must also end. Liberation is not of that kind.

Vedantic *sadhana* (discipline) can only remove your own ignorance; it does not bring a new thing, for *Brahman* is *here* and *now*.

...Those who say that by some effort in yoga you get *moksha*, try to introduce a new thing (*moksha*) which, having a beginning, must have an end. Production and destruction go together. Therefore yogic *moksha* is not true liberation. Not by *doing* anything can lasting, permanent liberation be realised. Similarly the endlessness of the soul in religion is illusory: Only the *Drg* is endless in the sense that we cannot truthfully speak of its appearing and disappearing.

When we say *Turiya* is realised or known, we mean only that *ignorance* is removed. The realisation is not the result of any activity, because *Turiya* was always there: [It is] only an unveiling.

...When the clouds pass, the moon is seen. No insight will reveal the moon of truth, only the passing of the clouds of ignorance. Hence there is no intuition or insight to be gained or matured, only a removal of something which obstructs...

The limitations and illusions of the world I have not seen anyone *else* impose on my mind. Therefore I must conclude that they are *self*-imposed. I am infinite, but in dream I impose the limitation on myself in the form of a tiger which I see there, but which is only my mind, i.e. myself. Similarly in waking I impose other limitations in the form of other objects and persons that are all really Me. Therefore constantly reflect and practice this exercise, viz: 'I am not limited by the body: I am unlimited.' Do not confine yourself to your own body.

...*Jnana* is to see that all things are the mind's own creations, that none are different from yourself, that none are other than the mind itself, and that therefore there is no *second* thing. But this you can get only by analysing the world during the waking state itself and finding it to be like a dream. This is why truth must be understood when awake, not in blank trance; when facing and seeing the world, not in negation of it.

The moment you know that the whole world is *Atman*, there is no snake [illusion]. If you know the Self, everything is only *Atman*. The world is *Atman*, but you have mistaken it for something else. You think you are imprisoned within this body, but really the Self, mind, *Atman*, awareness, is within and without the body. Hence widen your heart, mind, your self.

The teacher of *Brahman* dismisses everything as 'not this', '[this is] not *Brahman*', all the forms he mentions being superimposed on it, i.e. being mere words only, imaginations about it. The teacher means that, if you think dualistically, [i.e.] that *Brahman* is one [thing] and I am another, or that I (*Brahman*) is the soul and that (the body) is another, you will never understand it. The teacher's business is to show the seeker's foolishness in looking for *Brahman* as *other* than himself. More he cannot teach. The pupil must think [out the] rest for himself.

Atman is not a thing to be attained: It is always there, nearer than your body. No other effort is necessary than the *knowledge* of it.

10

The doctrine of non-causality

I N the study of truth ultimately there is no *karma* and no causality, but in the practical world they hold true.

You must differentiate between *immediate* cause and *ultimate* cause. It is the latter to which we refer in non-causality. The tree must have a seed as its cause, but now you are faced with the inability to trace any ultimate cause of the seed. The Advaitin admits fully the causal relation so far as this world is concerned, i.e. so far as it is not fully inquired into and as it is viewed by the ignorant.

How the seed grows into a mango tree, I have not seen, I do not know, says the Advaitin. At one time I see the seed, followed by a sprout. *How* the cause becomes the effect we do not see, but we see a *sequence* of water, when heated, changing into vapour. When did the seed cease to be the seed and become a plant? We do not see the two things at all. If I examine carefully, [if] I see carefully, I see only *Brahman*. (Did you see *how* your mind changed into the form of a mountain in your dream? Why are we not able to see the change? Because there *are* no two things, but mind or *Atman* alone.)

If there is no end to the causal series, as in the tree-seed chain, then does this not indicate there is a defect in the notion of causality itself?

You cannot get at the real cause of anything, nor at the whole series of its causes. You may say that quinine (cause) is the cure (effect) of malaria, but you cannot possibly explain all the factors *why* quinine cures malaria. When we say of a bird which cleverly builds its nest for the first time in its life, that it does so by 'instinct', [for] we cannot get the whole cause from physical factors alone. There is also its mind and what do we know of that? We explain nothing by 'instinct'. It is only a word, it is something which we imagine. We do not know the totality of conditions which are needed to bring about an event. All that you really know are your own *ideas*. What is behind or beyond your ideas you never know.

Things happen in a certain order, but this does not prove there is any causal connection between them, for the order is not invariable. We can say only that things *happen*: There is no such thing as a causal law. This uncertainty is what we mean by *maya*. For ideas cannot be grasped: They are gone before you can get hold of one. So it is impossible to bring them into connection causally. Bergson was right in saying there is only a continuous flow. This flow of indeterminate ideas is *maya*.

We do not deny that a succession of ideas, [that] objects appear before us. What we deny is that there is a causal relation between them.

The notion that the world is ever-changing precludes the notion of causality, because it proves that there is only one stuff or substance in all objects, the causal changes being illusory.

Causality is only an idea, nay imagination. There is
no such thing, but habit — not only in this life, but for
many lives — has so accustomed us to think causally,
that only the few can give up this illusion.

If you know the true meaning of causality, it is impossible to say there is such a thing as 'wrong' knowledge. If you know that everything is produced by the
mind, whether it be a mirage or the sun, then you always know everything 'correctly', i.e. as mental in nature, you will not get lost or confused in understanding the world. But those who are still in the stage of
causality, will get confused and say, 'The wall outside
is real, but the wall inside my mind is only an idea',
because they will seek a *cause* for the idea of the wall.
When you know there is no such thing as a causal relation, you will know that it is only the mind which
appears and disappears as objects, and it will then be
impossible to ask any questions, for all questions depend on the delusion of causality, the causal complex.
All is then known to be mind, all is unity. *Avidya* [ig-
norance] disappears, when causality is given up.

The fundamental principle of human thinking is
that no word can give a meaning, unless its opposite
is by its side. Misery is to be marked off from happi-
ness etc. This principle that all meanings run in du-
alities has a most important application in Vedanta,
for when applied to the notion of cause and effect, it
destroys the illusion of causality.

Those who ask, 'Why did I get this delusion of
the world?', do not understand that *because* they are
deluded, *because* they assume the truth of causality,

therefore they ask this question. They have already imagined there is an answer, when in fact there is no real problem. Nothing is produced or born, everything is already there as mind.

To be exact, we must say that nobody has ever seen a *jiva* [individual self] born; it is only our imagination. Did you see your own birth? 'But my present existence proves it.' No, your *existence* is not denied: We are discussing *birth*. 'But I have seen other people born?' Yes, that too is not being discussed: We are dealing with *you*, not others! Similarly you cannot be present at your own death and witness it. Therefore we say neither birth nor death can ever be proved. What is left? Only to *imagine* them! To say positively that you were aware of your body's birth is therefore to tell a lie; much less were you aware of the birth of your own self; and much less will your awareness of its death be possible. Objection: But everyone can see that a son is born to a father. Reply: We agree, but we are inquiring whether the *word* and *idea* 'birth' is true or not. We have found that they are mere words, imaginary things. There is no change really, only an imagination, an idea.

If A and B are in a causal relation, then A comes first, cause precedes effect. Now what do you see *first* of the external objects? Why, you see the *mental* impression of the same and nothing else at any time! Hence if the mental impression comes first, it must be a cause! This is my reply to the objection that the external world is the cause of our mental impression of it. No, there is *only* the mental impression as cause; there is nothing external in existence.

Objection is made to causality, because every idea must have an external experience or an external object to cause it, such as a pin to cause the pain of a pin-prick, or an elephant [which] must appear to cause its mental impression. Reply: This is also a criticism of idealism. It is the strongest argument of the realists, this one of pain caused by a physical instrument. We ask: Is the pain independent of the pin's point or has it gone out of it? What *is* pain? Is it something emerged from the pin or was it already in my body? If it came from the point, it must have existed in the pin. If it was in the body, then it could not have come from the cause (the pin). If the pin had not come into contact with the body, you would not have a pain. Did the pin drop the pain into the body? These questions are unanswerable so long as you set up a cause-effect duality... Huxley asked: Is the smell of the rose in your mind or in the rose at the time when you are smelling it? It is not possible to say it is either wholly. Only for language sake we say it is in the rose, but analysis finds it also in the mind, i.e. in yourself. We go to the cause (rose) *after* we are aware of the smell, *after* we have it in our own consciousness. Therefore we only *infer* the existence of the cause *after* having discovered smell — not in the cause, but in our own self. The rose is thus an *inference*, not a direct experience. Putting this in simpler language, we merely *imagine* a cause, the mind makes a construction of it. For what is an inferred and unseen cause (which is all you have, until the touch, sight, sensations arise) but an imagination? What does the mind do in this case? [It] forms an *idea*!

...Try to draw a line between your idea of the wall and the wall itself, between the *known* wall and the *existent* wall. The first is a *fact*, the second is a *supposition* between the believed cause and the believed effect. The truth is that the wall and the thought of it are one and the same, just as the thread and the cloth are the same. The one cannot exist apart from the other.

The Advaitins who say cause and effect are the same, identical, and there is no distinction between them, have gone high, but still have not reached the highest truth, which is that causality *itself* is only an idea, meaningless, imaginary and not really existent. Go to reality: You will not find cause and effect. The mind constructs it.

The hardest thing in Vedanta is to see that causation rises and falls with the ego. That is the last secret of Vedanta. When you see that the ego comes and goes, is [therefore] unreal, that mind alone is, then the ego is seen [to be] not other than mind, *no-two*, and the question of its cause and of a world cause simply does not and cannot arise.

No connection between *Drg* and *drsyam* has been proved. There is no causal relation between them.

There is nothing to show that there is any causal relation between two things, yet we start with the unconscious assumption that the relation is there and hence seek to *put* it there by imagination.

The causal idea works in you unconsciously as a hidden complex. Only the *mind* is present all the time.

Everything seen by it, whether objects or ideas, is still only mind and is not 'produced' or 'caused' by it.

Brahman can never be got by practice, whether yogic, *samadhi* etc. The reason is there is no such thing as a causal relation, hence no practice or effort will, as a cause, produce *Brahman* as an effect. A limited cause cannot produce an unlimited effect. *Brahman* is got by understanding only. But those who do not know the truth of non-causality will advocate yoga as a means of reaching *Brahman*; such is their ignorance.

Causality cannot operate when there is 'no-two'. Cause and effect mean *time*. At what *time* did the cause become an effect?

Why is *time* a question of such great importance? Because it involves the deeper problem of causality. The cause comes first and the effect subsequently, hence time must pass between them, if they do exist. Therefore, if time is shown to be illusory, then causality will have to be regarded as illusory too. When time collapses, causality collapses with it. That is why Kant put them together. Hence too the study of time should precede the study of causality.

The fallacy of causality is that we have to ask what is the cause for the ascertained given cause, and then again to ask what is the cause of that in turn? This leads us to an *infinite regress,* as with time. This is why Vedanta says causality does not explain anything in the final analysis.

All that we can accurately say of nature is that there are *sequences*. We cannot correctly say there is cause and effect.

11

Advaita in practice

Y ou can know *Brahman* only by *being* it.

Unity is *here* and *now*, always *has* been and always *will* be. But so long as man [remains] ignorant of this truth, he will only see variety.

The principle of unity alone can give you perfect satisfaction, as then you can have nothing taken away from you. What you [then] possess you will have until all eternity.

It is not enough to grasp the intellectual truth of non-duality: You must next fix your mind continually in it, i.e. you will get in glimpses at first, but you must not rest there. In order to become a *jnani* you should stabilize them through the constant reminder that the world is not separate from yourself. *Knowing* the *Atman* to be non-dual is the first stage, *realising* it as such is the second stage.

...Even the first single flash of understanding is true *jnana*, but it has passed away and you must seek its repetition constantly by such reflection, until the light stays fixed and does not depart. However, even after the first illumination you will never be mistaken again, for you will understand the true nature of things... You must keep the insight alive, no matter what you are doing. This demands constant concentration throughout the day, not merely sitting to meditate for half an hour. This flash is an absence of thought, like conscious sleep, where duality disappears. The first flash is the beginning of realisation and gradually ripens into full realisation. The process is to associate the insight gained by the first flash with everything that you do — eating, working, talking — with *Brahman*, until it becomes settled realisation…

Brahman must be realised in the *waking* state, when all objects are present to consciousness, otherwise it is nonsense.

…Where people cannot and do not think, they follow others. A *jnani* will see the world and get to know it is only an appearance. He is not blind; he sees every thing or object as it is, but he knows it is only an *idea*. Just as you see a mirage, the *jnani* sees the mirage of this world too, but he is not deceived by it.

So long as you are ignorant or a child, you will have the idea that God has created this world, because the causal notion will be there. Nobody wants suffering, and while the notion that suffering can be got rid of by appealing to God [persists], these wishes will sway the mind to believe in God. For them religion will arise, but for the man who wants *truth*, religion offers no consolation.

Yoga is a discipline through which one has to pass 'to make the mind clear', in the old Sanskrit phrase. If the mind is not strong enough to pursue truth, then yoga is prescribed to clarify and purify it. As a step, yoga or religion is welcome. But when advocated as being the highest, then it is a mistake.

All those who think philosophy is for theorizing, discussing, meditating, writing and studying only, have not understood it. Philosophy is to show men how to *live*: It is the most practical of things. It is primarily intended as a guide to action, for its final summing up (…) is to be always working for the welfare of all existence, not dreaming in a cave or *ashram*, or poring over metaphysical books. The only test of a philosopher is this: Is he able to sympathize with every other man who is suffering? Is he always trying to better the mental and material conditions of others? Such a test is clearly an implication of practical activity.

It is not enough to repeat Sanskrit wisdom like parrots, but it must be *lived*. And the highest test of it is the universal sympathy which it produces. The greater the true knowledge, the wider the sympathy, and as we rise higher, the less the distinctions which we make.

Advaita is finally to be judged from the point of view of the life we lead and not mere words; the practical good it can do rather than abstract discussions; the reasoned ethical guidance it can give rather than dogmatic injunction.

The more duality is disregarded in your actions and life, the clearer becomes realisation, the more you refrain from thinking of other people as separate from you, the more sympathetic to others that you are to them, the easier will realisation be possible…

There is no opportunity to develop your character, if you run away to a cave. The opportunity can come only, when you have to deal with others, i.e. in society. Most of those who run away are seeking personal satisfaction and fall deeper into the ego by this absence of opportunity to uplift or unselfishly help someone. There must be a second person present, i.e. in society, to permit you to unfold character.

Unless Vedanta promotes the well-being of *all*, it should be thrown away: This is the difference between it and all other philosophies. They may teach universal *brotherhood*, but this is quite different from the feeling of *oneness* in Vedanta. There are separate individuals in brotherhood, but none apart in oneness or identity.

Love and compassion for all mankind is the result of finding truth.

The real meaning of the doctrine of non-violence [*ahimsa*] is that if you harm others, it is equivalent to harming yourself.

Vedanta aims at the welfare of *all* beings, not only *human* beings.

Vedanta teaches that emotion and art are inseparable from life, that philosophy does not, cannot and should not take them away from us. What philosophy does is merely to *evaluate* both emotion and art and then remove the incorrect values we have placed upon them, substituting proper values in their place. It is thus not the Vedantic teaching that a philosopher should become unemotional, inartistic or incapable of enjoying beauty. He may be so, but he should know their value and place.

Philosophy is not different from life or from the world. Unless you treat all persons equally, there is no philosophy, hence it adopts the welfare of all the world and serves humanity. It is not merely a spinning of words: It is *truth*. The *jnani* sees every object and person as of the same essence as himself, the *Atman*.

First know what [the true nature of] this world is. Then see what sufferings [there] are. [Then] seek to free others from [their] suffering. Nature herself is forcing nations to realise the Vedantic social ideal of equality, sameness in all; that united they stand, but divided they collapse. This ideal means that everything is *Brahman*.

The immense practicality of Vedanta is hinted at in the *Upanishads* which assert that prosperity and peace can come to mankind only after it accepts the idea of its oneness. All other ways are illusory and will fail.

...The moment you make a distinction between yourself and another man, there is no Vedanta. The goal of Vedanta is to see the other man's sufferings as your own. Because in dream all the scenes and all the people are made of the same essence as yourself, they are as real as *you* are. Whatever *I* am, *you* are: I cannot be dissociated from you, the whole world is one. Do not treat other people as mere ideas, but your own self as real. If *they* are ideas, so are *you*; if *you* are real, so are *they*. Hence you must feel for them all just what you feel for yourself.

Death exists in order to teach man that the individual is but a *drsyam* which appears and disappears. Hence it is to urge him to seek immortal life.

Balance is the essential teaching of Vedanta. Thought must be balanced by action, solitude by service in society, nature by cities.

What is the fundamental reason why we should control the senses? Because their characteristic is to make you think erroneously that the second thing is *real*, that the objects are *real*.

If enjoyments come, keep your mind cool and controlled — level. Similarly with sorrows, for both will disappear in course of time. This means that you will still experience the joy or sorrow, but you won't get carried away by it. So long as you have a body, you must feel them. Yogis who sit for a hundred years to 'not feel' [them], are wasting their time. We are not stones. What is needed is the philosophical discrimination of their *value*, the mental analysis.

Attachment to objects means taking them to be real [permanent]. When attachment goes, *jnana* arrives.

It is the *attachment* to the form of separate objects which keeps you from apprehending their unity, not the *seeing* of them. How to think of both form *and* essence? By practice you must get to the stage where you can think of both simultaneously. This is done by knowing that the form is made of mind only. This requires sharp intelligence and constant repetition of practice of seeing both form and essence at the same time.

Only *truth* can give you the highest satisfaction. Unless you realise that everything is *in* you, there is no complete satisfaction.

There is no end in this world to desire. Satisfaction can come only from being satisfied with *Brahman*-knowledge which puts an end to all desires. All other desires are followed by further ones.

…The reason of hunger or desire lies in the memory of the past satisfaction of the hunger or desire. This is repeated continuously. This is the process of the *vasanas* [ingrained tendencies]. There is no new creation really, the *vasanas* cause you to repeat the desires. Repeated imagination makes you a slave of the desire which has been re-echoed from the past; the desire is only imagination deeply rooted. Thus *karma* is created. When a man realises at last that his desires are only *ideas*, he is able to get rid of them. Until then they will go on repeating themselves.

…If *maya* did not exist, there would be no incentive, no purpose in seeking for reality, *Brahman*. Hence it may be taken as a meaning of the world that all these forms exist to enable us to reflect on them and find the Mind, the non-dual Reality of which they are mere appearances.

Those who say or think, 'In the course of time I shall gain knowledge, heaven etc.', cannot gain truth, for they are *now* the inhabitants of truth and have not to gain it. They are ignorant, for they expect change in that where there is and can be no change. They think they are *going* to change, because they are attached to body and personality. This is their illusion.

...When asked whether there is a God, we keep quiet, because no proof is available of his existence, and therefore all such discussion with believers — not thinkers — is useless. Not that we are atheists: We start with agnosticism and we come to believe in a God not concocted by men, but as He is in *truth*.

Brahman is silence. Knowing that, you need not enter into discussion if you want to get at truth, for words are only words, ideas. But to *refute* others we may use words. [However,] in the verbal expression of every position that can be taken up, including ours, there is contradiction... In the final stage of argument *jnana* can only show that both he and the opponent are limited by contradiction in every word and sentence. Give up the misleading and impossible idea that you are going to establish *Brahman* by means of books, writings, speech and other words. All you can do is to *refute* other people's arguments about *Brahman*. He who has realised *Brahman* has nobody to argue with, because there is then only *one*, no second person than himself.

...Wherever the mind goes, whatever object you see, whatever thought you hold, you will know that in essence it is all one and the same thing. You will go to the very root of the matter and discover it to be mind, and mind to be *Brahman*. The body may remain as an object, whose continuously changing nature you know and remember, whereas the *Atman* will be for you the Ever-stable. Therefore there is nothing to be given up: You will see *Brahman without a second thing.* You will understand that, as in dream, your own mind appears as the various scenes you behold, so your own nature, *Brahman*, is appearing before you as all this world...

...The moment you remove *maya*, identify yourself with your real nature — 'that you are *Brahman*' — then you attain everything. If everything is *Brahman*, how can you then desire anything? Everything is contained *in* you: There *is* nothing else. It includes all blessings, nothing more is required...

'Ever-peaceful' means you do not want anything, not even God or heaven, because you know that even heaven and God are *in* you.

12

The *jnani*, the knower of truth

THE *jnani* knows that the reality is *himself*, that the world which is seen is only an appearance.

A true *jnani* can never renounce anything, it is impossible. He has only renounced the idea of a *separate* universe.

It is utterly impossible according to the *Brihadaran-yaka* [*Upanishad*], *Vivekachudamani*, for anyone to detect who is a *jnani*. No outward sign will reveal it. The nearest but partial possible test given in the [*Bhagavad*] *Gita*, *Ashtavakra* [*Samhita*] and *Mandukya* [*Upanishad*] is: Is he doing good to others without thought of gaining benefit for himself?…

If the *jnani* is able to eat, work and attend to practical duties without losing his *jnana*, why should he not be able to sleep and dream like other men without losing his *jnana*? And this is the case.

The *jnani* will follow whatever occupation he wishes according to the circumstances. There are no prohibitions for him. He may be a coachman or a king.

The *jnani*, on attaining realisation, will not give up his vocation in life, but will continue it as before. If he was a king, he continues so; if a palanquin bearer, he will remain one. In short he still does his duty, but now it is done with the motive for the good of others.

Jnanis have lived in the company of butchers, shop-keepers, hunters, even robbers, behaving as they did, not claiming to be different from them, but occasionally dropping some word, giving some hint or advice, which will ever so slightly give higher ideals to his companions. Thus he will instill hope into seekers' hearts that it is really possible to attain higher levels.

...A *jnani* knows the external world is *Atman*, whereas ordinary man does not know, yet both live and work in the world in the same way. There is no outside difference to be detected between a *jnani* and the ordinary man: The difference is entirely *inside* the mind.

You cannot say how a *jnani* dresses or moves or works: He is trackless like a fish in water...

The infallible test of a false *jnani*, where there is no other way of testing him, is whether he is actively engaged in removing the suffering of others and serving humanity.

The *jnani's* idea of service will comprehend that, whilst he tries to relieve physical suffering, to remove ignorance is still higher and a more necessary service.

The *jnani* makes no voluntary effort, but does what has to be done. Therefore he will practise both activity and abstention at different times.

The sage will live as he pleases, above codes. But this does not mean he will do wrong, harm others or cause suffering. For his self-identification with them will prevent this.

The enlightened man does not criticize or praise *men*, but he does criticize or praise *actions*. He does not speak ill of persons, but he must condemn or discourage or praise or support wrong or right actions...

The minds of those who judge a *jnani*, act on the consistency theory. Hence they judge him incorrectly.

Whatever happens to the wise, whether it be success or failure, pain or pleasure, he will think on every occasion that it is *Brahman* and thus lift himself above material experiences.

The *jnani's* mind is paradoxically more active and less active than the ordinary man's. More active because he uses his brains, less active because whatever happens, he remains unworried and unaffected. He knows the past is gone and won't worry over it. If present losses occur, he knows that all is still *Brahman* and hence nothing is really lost.

The *jnani* sees and knows the table as a table, but at the same time he knows that it is only *Brahman*.

There is no distinction between 'unreal' and 'real' for the *jnani*, only for the student. Hence in seeing the table, he knows he sees *Brahman*. It is not a question of seeing a table first and then interpreting as *Brahman*.

To the *jnani* both death and rebirth are ideas and hence do not exist in reality. Do not ask him therefore what is going to happen after death, because the question is meaningless to him. Everything is but mind, ideas to him.

When I know all is *Brahman*, I can help an other who is suffering, because I consider him as myself and consider that I am suffering in *him*. I see a second person — duality — but I know as a *jnani* that he is the same person as myself. If everyone sympathised with everyone else, then *jnana* would have been universal. A *jnani* knows the truth and always acts to help others, whereas ordinary man may or may not help others. The *jnani* knows all life is one, ignorant man does not. That is the difference between them.

This realisation in its fullness brings absolute harmony between thought and action and makes the *jnani*.

About the Author

V. Subrahmanya Iyer was born in 1869 in Salem, Tamil Nadu, South India, from Brahminical parentage. After studying in Madras and in Bangalore, specializing in mathematics and physics, he went on to teach sciences, first in Agra and from 1895 in Mysore. He received initiation into classical Advaita Vedanta from Swami Satchidananda Shivabhinava Narasimha Bharati (1858-1912), the then head of Sringeri Math, one of the four monasteries founded by Sri Shankaracharya. In 1920 Iyer, registrar of the University of Mysore and gifted with a brilliant intellect, became the personal tutor to the Maharaja of Mysore, Sri Krishnaraja Wodiyar IV (1884-1940), the renowned sage-sovereign who had founded the University in 1916. This office he held until the Maharaja's death without, however, accepting any form of remuneration. In 1932, at the instigation of the Maharaja who took a keen interest in the dissemination of Vedantic ideas and ideals, the Mysore Circle of Vedantic Studies was started. Here Iyer was to train scholars and, in particular, many monks of the Ramakrishna Order in the intricacies of Vedanta philosophy and allied subjects.

One of those who frequented Iyer's classes was an Englishman, Paul Brunton (1898-1981), the well-known writer, traveler, mystic and philosopher, who has done much to bridge the philosophical and spiritual heritage of Orient and Occident. With the appearance of his book, 'A Secret Search in India' (1934), Ramana Maharshi (1879-1950), the silent sage of Arunachala, was to become known to the world at large. Brunton became Iyer's student and associate for many years, and the present selection of teachings owes its origin to the notes taken down by him.

In 1937 Iyer traveled to Paris as the sole Indian delegate to the 9th International Congress of Philosophy, organized by the University of Paris. While in Europe he gave lectures in various countries and was able to meet with such notable figures as Henri Bergson and Carl Gustav Jung. V. Subrahmanya Iyer passed away in 1949 in Mysore after an active life wholly dedicated to a philosophy inclusive of all forms of knowledge: the Philosophy of Truth.

www.ingramcontent.com/pod-product-compliance
Lightning Source LLC
Chambersburg PA
CBHW022306060426
42446CB00007BA/733